Club Syndication

How the Wealthy Raise Money and Invest in Commercial Real Estate

Shane Melanson

This book is designed to provide reliable and competent information regarding the subject matter. However, it is sold with the understand that the author and publisher are not engaged in rendering financial, legal, or other professional advice. Laws and practices of investing in real estate vary from state to state, province to province and country to country, and if legal assistance is required- you should seek the services of a professional. The author and professional specifically disclaim and liability that is incurred from the use or application of the contents of this book.

Club Syndication

Here's What's Inside…

Introduction

I grew up in Whitecourt, Alberta, a small logging town in northern Alberta. Both my parents were teachers, and growing up, I was not surrounded by investors or businesspeople for mentors. I did have a few friends with parents who were entrepreneurial. I noticed those friends had more 'toys' than we did; boats, dirt bikes, bigger homes, nicer cars and went on trips to Mexico or Hawaii every year- things you would expect from wealthier people.

I had just graduated from high school and was working for my friends' father. They owned a logging company, and in the summer, I'd build logging roads for them. My friend, who was five years older than me, was always into new business ideas and opportunities. By the end of summer, after four months of working with his dad, I'd saved up $13,500 for University. My friend told me about an opportunity he was making money in and asked if I wanted to invest the money I'd saved for school, with him. He described the unbelievable returns I'd make investing with him. Being an 18-year-old and seeing how rich he was, I thought it would be smart to trust him and put my money next to his. I put everything I made that summer, all $13,500 into his investment. For 18 years old, it was a lot of money.

At the time, my dad was a principal, and mom taught Grade 1. They heard about my investment and that a few other wealthy business owners in Whitecourt were putting money into this opportunity. Not wanting to miss out, my dad remortgaged their house to participate in the investment. My parents had just paid it off and were mortgage free. They took out a $100,000 new mortgage against their home and invested in the opportunity, they believed would be lucrative.

Six months went by and we don't hear a thing. No mention of when we'll start to see returns. I start to get concerned about the investment. As time passed, and more excuses on why things were taking longer (complications with the deal, banking holdups, and on and on), it should have become clear, we were not going to see our money again. The funny thing is, as I look back, it took several years for us to come to grips with the fact that our money was gone. It's difficult to accept that you've made such a massive mistake.

This lesson was a tough pill for me to swallow. It taught me lessons on how not to invest, and how some people use greed to lure others, especially hard-working individuals that don't have much experience investing, into deals they shouldn't be investing in.

Teachers, Doctors, Dentists and Accountants do not buy and sell real estate every day. How could they be expected to understand how these investments are structured, or the risks involved in these opportunities? When my parents invested, no one said; *"Gerry, you could lose it all. Are you sure you want to remortgage your home to invest in this speculative deal?"*

Fast-forward to today: my career is centered around investing in commercial real estate and helping others do the same. With my partners, I've raised more than $20 million in various investments (called 'Syndications').

It's a much different conversation when a sophisticated, high-net-worth individual is considering an investment versus, what I would call, smaller, retail investors ('mom and pop') who typically invest less than $50,000. My passion is in educating anyone looking to invest in real estate deals. Given where I came from and my past experiences, **my goal is to protect and empower average, hard working individuals to assess the risks involved in investing, specifically as it relates to real estate opportunities.**

I'd like to do this by outlying the steps and skills required for those serious about raising money to pursue their goal of growing wealth investing in commercial real estate.

Warren Buffett's #1 Rule: "**<u>Don't Lose Money</u>**".

For those who are actively investing in real estate, I want to show you how to raise money the right way. When I see the guru's proclaiming how they raise money- I don't agree with many of their traditional methods. There is far too much risk for the average investor in many of these structures. It's certainly not how the high-net-worth or ultra-wealthy invest.

Even though I started with a negative investment experience, I was fortunate to find two great mentors who taught me how to invest in real estate and raise money the right way.

In the following pages you'll read about those experiences. Enjoy the book.

I hope it inspires you to take the time to understand the responsibility that goes into investing in commercial real estate and raising money. Remember you are dealing with people's livelihoods, they're putting a tremendous amount of faith and trust in you.

There is a high responsibility that goes along with raising money. The people who are most successful at raising money are far more careful with others' money than they are their own.

They treat it with extreme care and attention. It's an important distinction many investors ignore.

To your financial freedom!

Shane

Club Syndication (How to Raise Money and Invest in Commercial Real Estate Like the Ultra-Wealthy)

There's a reason why ultra-wealthy have upwards of 25% of their net worth invested in cash flowing commercial real estate. Real estate is a durable, secure and tangible, hard asset.

Professional commercial real estate investors dominate in three specific areas: they see the best properties first, they attract capital (both debt and equity) and they have experienced teams to manage and oversee the operations.

For the average person looking to invest in commercial real estate, they quickly discover how capital-intensive it is. Then, they find it's difficult to find the quality assets to buy.

Investing in commercial real estate is seldom taught to outsiders. It can take years working in the business to fully understand the moving parts and avoid the common pitfalls. Having expert local knowledge is key- but finding people you can trust for that information is not done on the internet or by calling a for sale or for lease sign.

This is why the best commercial real estate is concentrated in the hands of a few ultra-wealthy investors or owned by large publicly traded companies.

This is the reason I wrote this book. To help those who want to invest in commercial real estate, to do it like the ultra-wealthy. I help investors just like you find the best properties first. I give you to the tools and strategies needed to raise the money to purchase these assets, so you can start to invest like the wealthy. This is not a get rich quick gimmick. Investing in commercial real estate takes time, patience, money and a deep skill set. But, when done right, just one property can help set you up for financial independence.

The biggest mistake I see most beginners in real estate make: they stay too small for too long because they think investing in commercial real estate is too risky. Or, they don't believe they have the knowledge to invest in commercial real estate. But when you see how the ultra-wealthy invest in what I call "**Club Syndications**" you'll see how it's possible for the average person to.

Club Syndication: "*is a small group of people that pool their money to purchase larger commercial real estate properties*".

Generally, one person in the group has commercial real estate experience and knowledge, finds the best properties and in exchange, is paid a fee and receives a % ownership in the property. This book will explain the skills needed to find the properties and raise the capital needed to set up your own Club Syndication and become a professional commercial real estate investor.

If you'd like more information, visit: **www.ClubSyndication.com** and get additional resources on how to find properties, analyze deals and tools and examples of how to raise money for your opportunities.

Deal Flow (The Reason 'Club Syndications' Are Used by the Ultra-Wealthy to Buy Commercial Real Estate)

There are three main components to investing in real estate, whether it's commercial or residential. The first is **finding the deal**. Then you need to **fund the deal** (raise the money, both equity and debt). The last component is the **follow-through or execution** (property management, operations and exit).

It doesn't need to be any more complicated than that.

In my experience, most real estate investors take the traditional path, starting small, as I did.

I started buying and flipping single-family homes, then moved up to building spec houses, increasing the level of sophistication and risk. As I gained investing knowledge, my profits increased and so did the size of my deals.

My goal was to eventually invest in commercial real estate. I got a job working at Sun Life Financial, as commercial lender. It was there I was exposed to how investors bought and financed multimillion-dollar deals.

It was at Sun Life, that I was exposed to my first mentor. Jim D taught me how money worked in commercial real estate, how lenders viewed risk and what amount of debt they would be prepared to lend, based on certain basic principles.

Debt makes up anywhere from 50% to 80% of the money needed to purchase a property. The remainder comes from equity- cash. Equity is where high-net-worth (HNW) individuals or investors, enter a transaction.

When it comes to commercial real estate and larger deals, even the very rich typically invest in **"Club Syndications."**

A Club Syndication usually consists of between 4 to 20 individuals. Usually, one or two in the club have experience investing in commercial real estate. The other club members ride along, passively. Those with experience investing generally get paid a fee, to put the deal together, raise the money and oversee the investment.

It's a smart way of diversifying against risk and of **increasing deal flow** (ability to see multiple deals and get involved in them simultaneously).

These Clubs can purchase multiple properties because they're able to raise enough money from their group to attract sellers. They have the liquidity (cash available) to buy multiple properties.

Compare that to one high net worth individual, like a doctor, dentist, or business owner who has $1 million to $2 million to invest. For most commercial properties, this would require all their cash. Once they pull the trigger on a property, they're out of cash and need to wait until they can earn enough, save and then deploy again.

The challenge with this approach, is deal flow slows down. One of the core principles in commercial real estate (unlike residential) is that investors be the first to see deals. And, the best way to first in line to see subsequent deals, is to close on existing deals.

I just worked with a doctor who purchased his first retail property. He invested most of his liquid cash and is eager to get into the next property. He's now getting calls from lots of brokers and sellers all showing him deals.

His ability to buy the next property is constrained by his ability to raise the necessary equity. So, I showed him the same strategies I use to raise $1M-$5M for good, well performing commercial real estate opportunities.

The key thing to know, as an investor buying commercial real estate, is that once you show the market you can close- you will ***attract deal flow***. For the next three to six months you'll be on the radars of brokers and owners in their market.

But, if you're resources are dry and you go away for two years, you're forgotten. You don't see deals first and you start the cycle over again.

Having been an investor and agent selling commercial real estate, I discovered that the people who see the best opportunities first are those who have the most capital, close and do so without too much brain damage (*stress*).

 They are the professionals who buy and sell on a frequent basis. Brokers are only paid when a property sells. So, they show the best properties to those who will close first. Even owners, looking to see their property ***off-market***, know who the active buyers are and call them first.

In commercial real estate- deal flow and seeing a property early (or first) is how you win.

Domino Effect (How the Wealthy Raise Money to Invest in Commercial Real Estate)

In this book I want to focus on raising capital and finding opportunities. Most courses and books discuss one or the other. Knowing how to find opportunities is great, but if you can't fund it- what's the point? And if all you know how to do is raise money but can't find opportunities or assess a deal, then you can lose money quickly.

Investing starts once you find an opportunity. But, if you don't have the confidence and the understanding of how to fund them, you won't act. Too many investors new to commercial real estate play small, looking at residential or small commercial properties that just aren't going to generate the cash flow and returns required to achieve financial independence.

It's not until you get to the next level of investing, where you understand how to raise money properly, that you can start taking advantage of the investing network effect- **money attracts deals**. Simple as that. Just follow the money, and you will see the best deals.

Brokers and sellers follow the money- which is why you want to know how to raise capital.

Once you're on an upward trajectory of finding better deals, it makes it easier to raise money. You can see there's a network effect- the more money you have/raise, the more opportunities you see and the better these opportunities are. As you become the 'go-to' buyer in a market, investors with money, come to you and want to be part of your deals. So, raising money becomes easier.

This is where you see professional investors, who have been at it for years and who have developed a reputation for raising money, closing and delivering returns to their investors are able to make millions each year investing in commercial real estate.

Finding the property is first. But, if you don't understand how to raise money, then you won't pull the trigger. You'll end up with a reputation as someone who puts properties under contract, but never closes. In the industry, they're called *'flakes'*.

Success in this business comes down to your ability to raise money effectively and find great properties to close on.

The Five-Part Capital-Raising Framework

These are the five strategies and mindsets the ultra-wealthy use to leverage their wealth to buy more and of the best commercial properties-while mitigating their risks.

Step One:
Controlling Deals

Step one of The Five-Part Capital-Raising Framework starts with finding and controlling a *'live'* property for sale.

In 2012, I put together a team to buy multifamily (MF) buildings in Texas. I had experience in Houston and Dallas and was excited to take what I'd learned and start acquiring 200+ unit apartment complexes.

Initially, I started raising capital. I went out to my investors and larger equity players in the US who wanted to own MF properties. We identified several MF options in the market and put together our investment packages to raise funds.

I thought, because we were looking at real deals in the market, if we could get the money, we'd be in business. So, I wanted to make sure I had money in the bank to be able to take down these large MF deals (ranging from $15M - $45M).

Each meeting would essentially end the same way, with a question from the person with money: "*so, do you have this MF property under contract*"?

Me*: No, I don't.*

Investor: *Come back when you have the property under contract*- meaning, when you control the deal we can talk. Otherwise, this meeting and this deal is all hypothetical, because for all you know someone else might have it under contract.

We had an incredible investor pitch deck (marketing materials), a solid team that understood the markets- but investors wanted to know we had **live deals under control**. There was no sense talking about a property that could be sold to someone else in the time it would take to put it under contract.

Investors were not interested in theoretical discussions, of what we could do when we bought a property. High net worth individuals and the ultra-wealthy are pitched '*ideas*' all the time. They want to know you, the investor, is real.

Investors want to see a property under contract. The term some investors use is to describe a deal under contract and ready to be pitched to investors, is a deal is fully '*baked*'.

Learning from this lesson, we put the first property under contract, a 182-unit MF in Houston. Now our investor meetings got real. We got down to brass tacks regarding what the investor wanted (returns, control) and whether the deal we had under contract was something that fit and matched their risk threshold.

It all starts with finding the opportunity and underwriting it to make sure it fits the plan you have. If the deal passes these hurdles, it's time to put it under contract- starting with an LOI (Letter of Intent).

One common oversight for new investors raising money, is they don't consider alternatives places people can put their money? Commercial real estate isn't the only asset class investors looks at. Some investors like the stock market because stocks are liquid. Others like bonds because bonds are liquid and can provide stable (albeit lower) returns.

Understanding investors have multiple options, you can speak to the reasons why investing in commercial real estate is the right thing to do for them.

The investors will enjoy predictable monthly cash flow, appreciation over time, advantageous tax benefits, and hedges against inflation in the future.

I also like to investigate my competition, specifically what other professional investors (or club syndicators) in my market are offering when they raise money. What properties are they buying? What returns are they giving investors?

You'll find once you enter the commercial real estate market, even in big cities, there are generally a handful of people doing deals consistently. Studying what they do and how they do it, is important to know. It's likely the investors you're talking to, will also be seeing your competition's deals. So, you want to be sure that you understand what deals they're looking at, how they are structured and what type of fees and returns they are offering.

Finding the property, putting it under contract and understanding the competition all impact your ability to raise money. The more you study and research your market, the more confidence you'll have when you ask an investor to come into your deal.

As you build your track record of successful deals, raising money gets easier. If you don't have a track record, then you will likely give investors a higher % of the deal. That's ok. Commercial real estate is a long game. As you gain experience and credibility, you'll be able to dictate more favourable terms for your investments. But starting out, it's ok to give up more to your investors. They are taking a risk on you and should be compensated.

Leveraging your team who has a track record is one other way you can increase the likelihood of raising money if you're new. Surround yourself with the best team, one with a proven track record. Show your investors why you're the right person (or team) to invest with. For instance, do you have predictable cash flow each month, a great asset in a great location, ...

Understand your investors wants and needs.

More on this later.

Step Two:
Structuring Your Deal

The best way to think about structuring a deal is in terms of what you are prepared to give to an investor, so they will give you money. The higher the risk, the more the investor will expect.

Risk in a deal is calculated a few different ways. The 3 main risks are:

1. Market Risk (jobs, GDP, political)

2. Deal Risk (is this a good property)

3. Team Risk (who is doing the deal)

The way I structure deals is by offering investors a preferred return first, which is money an investor receives before me. A preferred return could be anywhere from 6% for a very low-risk investments to upwards of 12% for higher-risk developments.

The following is how I raise money. It's not to say this is the right way or the only way- just a proven way I do it.

Before we begin, there are two important terms I should clarify:

General Partners (GP) and **Limited Partners** (LP). A General Partner (GP) is the principal in the deal, the person putting it all together. The GP will find the property, raise the money (equity and debt) and oversee the management. A GP can be one person or a small group.

A Limited Partner (LP)can also be one person or multiple people. When there are multiple LP's, the structure is called a 'Syndicate'. In most cases, LP's in private syndications are high-net-worth individuals and accredited investors. LP investments, in properties I purchase raise money from investors anywhere from $50,000 to $1 million.

If an LP invests $100,000, for example, and is offered a 6% preferred return, they would get the first $6,000 return before the GP would participate in the upside.

After that initial preferred return (6% example), there's the split. To make the math easy we'll say 70% goes to the LP, and 30% goes to the GP. That means anything after the 6% is split 70/30. If $100,000 was raised, and in year one there's a $10,000 distribution, $6,000 of that $10,000 would go to the LP off the top. Seventy percent of the remaining $4,000 ($2,800) would go to the LP, and $1,200 would go to the GP.

That's a simple and high-level way you could structure a LP/GP deal. There are multiple ways to structure these deals, with waterfalls, and different splits once initial equity is returned to LP's. But, if the offering is too complicated, I've found investors get nervous. A confused mind says no. So, it's best to keep the structure simple to explain and fair to your investors.

There are other important elements inside the structure that need to be identified; I'll touch on a few of them. To fully understand these terms, it's best to get legal advice and go to Google for definitions.

When a GP acquires a property, they earn an **acquisition fee** (ranging from 1-3% of purchase price); a **disposition fee** (from 1% to 3%); and an **asset-management fee** (3-5% of the Gross Income).

When a GP charges the asset management fee it is to oversee the property, take care of the bookkeeping and accounting and to ensure the property is performing. Investing in Commercial real estate is not a passive activity – especially if there is a value-add component. An important distinction: asset management does not mean property management. Asset manager is strategic, while the property manager is hands-on, day-to-day.

GP's will secure the debt and, if you (the GP) are providing a guarantee, you may look to charge a fee for that (0.5 – 1%).

Some LP/GP structures will offer '***Waterfall Payouts***', which are essentially hurdle rates. For example – if the **hurdle rate** (preferred return) is 10%, the GP might get a higher % of the profits once a hurdle has been achieved. The next hurdle rate could be 15%, after which the GP participates even more in the upside. Waterfalls are designed to incentivise the GP to increase the profitability of a property (performance-based compensation).

In every investment- you MUST have both Legal and Tax advice. A lawyer will help you paper your Limited Partnership Agreement. That will include the accredited investor forms that your investors need to fill out, your prospectus (or Offering Memorandum, OM), the marketing materials you show investors (a Pitch Deck), and any collateral you give prospective investors. You need to understand what you can say and what is not allowed, including required disclaimers. You need to know who you can and cannot show this to regarding the marketing of your opportunities. If you've never done any of this, it's beneficial to sit down with a lawyer or understand the laws. All provinces and countries have different regulations with respect to how you raise money.

I've learned expensive lessons structuring deals the wrong way for investors.

Tax structuring is the next critical piece of the puzzle. How do you distribute funds to your investors?

A development project, which is being sold will be taxed differently than an income producing asset which expected to be more passive in nature.

There are a numerous tax and legal considerations. Many new investors put all their focus on raising money, without much thought to the legal or tax implications. It's a costly mistake, that can haunt your deal after you close if it's structured incorrect. You don't need to be the legal or tax expert, but you should have them on your team (by team, I mean- you pay them for their services, they are not part of the GP).

How to Raise money from your LP's?

I am a firm believer in complete transparency of how, I the GP will be compensated. My goal is to align my interests and the LP's interests. Which means, GP's don't make money unless the LP's are paid first.

Investors don't like to see GP's getting rich off fees while they, the LP are holding the risk. LP's want to be shoulder to shoulder with the GP; if they're not making money, you shouldn't be either.

<u>I would never invest in a deal where the GP did not have skin in the game</u>. Every time I see a deal where the GP is not putting in equity, I know it's destined for failure.

Skin in the game doesn't need to be 20% or 30% of the total equity- but the GP, in my opinion, should have enough money in the deal that they'd feel significant pain if things don't perform. In real estate, deals take time. Markets change, and you want to make sure the GP will stick around for the long-haul. If things don't work out as planned, the GP is there to work it out.

I've seen markets go up and drop several times in my investing carer. I live in Calgary, Alberta and did a deal in Muskoka, Ontario, which is just north of Toronto. It's a four-hour flight and a two-hour drive to get to Muskoka from Calgary.

I spent between two and four weeks at a time away from my family (120 to 160 days a year) to work on a project because things didn't go as planned. We had to raise additional capital from our investors, which is never easy, but was required to execute our game plan.

Our investors saw that we were doing everything possible to make the deal a success, even though it had not performed the way we or they had anticipated. I was essentially living at the property, making sales, getting the development, talking to counselors, and doing everything possible to make the deal a success.

In the end, it was a success. Three-and-a-half years of a tremendous amount of hard work from the GP's and our team. In this investment, we purchased the properties for $8.5 million and we sold for $17 million. We paid our investors several million dollars at the end of the deal, plus money they earned throughout. It was a huge success for our LP's. As GPs, because it took longer and required more capital than we anticipated, we didn't profit as well as we planned. But, this is part of investing in commercial real estate. Our LP's trust us more and know that we'll be there for them when things are challenging.

Today, when I raise money for a property, the people I talk to, know, from experience, that I'm going to do whatever it takes to make the investment a success. There's no question of whether I'll stick around if the deal doesn't go as smoothly as planned.

When you're new to the game, this will be a concern your investors have. They may not voice it- but it will be there. Many investors have been burned by deals that went off the rails. In some cases, by a GP not sticking around. It's unfortunate, but it's a reality. As a GP, having skin in the game keeps your feet to the fire.

Quantifying the risk in a deal is critical.

Astute investors are smart and understand there is risk in every opportunity. If you sugar-coat it or try to avoid answering questions about what can hurt them, sophisticated investor will see through it and lose confidence in you. I prefer to talk about these risks before an investor even asks. Don't 'hope' an investor isn't thinking it. Tell them, instead, how you see the risks and your plan to mitigate them.

As a GP gains experience, the risk of execution goes down. With more experience, a GP can demand higher fees and percentages. However, if you're starting out, and don't have a long track record, you'll want to incentivize your investors to invest with you. You may need to give them higher returns and splits in the beginning to take the initial risk. As you gain experience and a track record, you gain confidence and control over how much upside you keep.

A big danger I see being taught to new investors by veterans- is that a newbie investor should structure their deals the same way as professional investors. It doesn't make sense. Someone with 20 years' experience and a long successful track record should be paid more than someone who is getting into investing and raising money for the first time. Trying to keep too much money in the deal, or 'fee your partners' to death is a sure-fire way to spin your wheels and raise little to no money.

Just look at Shark Tank or Dragon's Den. How often new business owners trying to raise money with an unproven or an infant business look to raise money by offering 5 or 10% of their business to the Sharks. They get nowhere. On the other hand, those businesses with sales and proven track record for success have the Sharks and Dragons' fighting to invest. It will be the same thing when you go out and raise capital for your investments.

Step Three: Positioning

Step three of The Five is positioning. You, the principal or the general partner, are the expert and the authority, must be knowledgeable, as a trusted expert and a master of the asset class you're entering.

"Asset class" could be multi-family, retail, industrial, office, or mobile homes. In the initial stages, it's difficult to understand and be a master at multiple asset classes. Over time, you'll likely be exposed to different assets and when you have a solid team in place, you can look at deals outside your area of expertise.

In the 15 years I've invested in real estate (10 in commercial), I've been fortunate to have experience with mobile homes, apartment buildings, retail, and industrial and land.

I'm not proficient in office deals or hotels and would not, at this stage, raise money to invest in an asset class I didn't understand or have a partner that understood it.

I've invested in a portfolio of mortgages, which was a great opportunity, but a tonne of work.

The more you're positioned as the expert in an asset class, the more experience and context you can draw on when looking at properties. If it's the first time you're looking at a retail property-there will be many unknowns for you. If you've bought and sold 10 retail properties, you'll start to know what tenants want, what makes a retail property a success or a failure. All the experience you gain with each property will give you confidence and, your investors' confidence in you to make them money.

Being someone with a deep understanding of an asset class, means you know how money is made, the demand from tenants, the risks and threats of new supply, and sensitivity for rents. You understand how supply and demand factors will impact your opportunity.

So, how do you start?

Before I ever pitch an investor, I make sure I've driven the property several times and understand it and the market. I look at the surrounding real estate as well. I've probably talked to businesses in the area and owners. I have conversations with banks, so I know how much debt I'll be able to get from them and what terms they're looking for. I've talked to brokers in the area, so I understand rents. I ask about absorption and any new developments coming online.

Before I talk to investors, I have become an expert on that property, so when investors ask me questions, I'm confident in my ability to describe why I like this opportunity. If I'm sitting down with them, I'll pull out my phone and show them pictures of the property and explain the metrics of the deal.

It really circles back to: <u>finding the property</u>. If you don't have a great property, that you understand - it's tough to be the authority. Experienced investors with money can sense if you're an expert or faking it.

I had a conversation with a gentleman who wants to organize a syndication to invest in commercial real estate. He likes industrial properties and said he had a deep understanding of the Calgary market. So, to test him, I asked: what are you seeing with market rents? What about vacancy in the NE, vs SE or S industrial market? Do you know what absorption is over the past 12 months or what new developments are coming on? What sector of industrial are you looking at? Manufacturing, distribution, storage, small bay, condominium? Do you know the cost to construct new industrial? What about site coverages or parking? He had no idea.

I explained, that when we look at raising money to invest, we become an expert in all of this and then some. It may seem overwhelming- but a few lunches, reading market reports and driving you market with a clipboard, camera and pen and you can become well versed in a few weeks.

Because commercial real estate is an inefficient market, and the information is not centralized, it's difficult to be an expert sitting at home. It requires getting out and talking to people. This means, you'll be building relationships with industry professionals.

And, it's important to understand that these professionals have taken years to learn and study the market. They are not going to share it with unknown and unproven investors. So, first, you're looking to find the right people to talk to. Then, you build relationships with them. And, understand, these professionals only get paid when they sell a property- it's important to let them know you're serious and will not try and go around them. Too often new investors don't understand the rules of buying real estate and violate unwritten rules. I'll give you a good rule to follow here: <u>If an agent shows you a deal- you owe it to that agent to use them if you are not already represented.</u> If you are being represented, then be upfront with the agent.

Next, let's talk about **attraction marketing**. Ideally, you want people (investors and brokers with properties) to come to you.

The traditional way of raising money was not necessarily cold-calling, but you would call or email investors to set up meetings with them. While I still do this, I've found with more experience and knowing my desired outcome for each meeting, I'm able to steer the conversation with investors in the direction I want. My goal is growing and expanding my network. Which means, for every investor I make money for, I want them to introduce me to good people they think would benefit from investing in my deals. If I am raising money from someone who is in a certain industry or sector, I want to create a situation where they feel comfortable and want to invite their friends to hear about my investment.

There are strict guidelines you must follow when you're discussing investment opportunities with new people. It is CRITICAL you consult a lawyer and understand the different rules and laws around this.

Ok, let's assume you have done your legal due diligence and you're raising money.

I like to meet new investors for coffee or lunch a few times. As much as you want to raise money, you don't want to take money from people who will be a pain in the ass. One of the biggest mistakes I see new investors make is to raise money from anybody who will give it to them. Then they deal with the headache of phone calls every week and investors asking, "What's happening?" and, "I need my money out," or, "I'm getting a divorce."

Some deals take a few years where others can be 10+ years to exit. If you take on investors who aren't stable in their businesses or at home, they can create real challenges for you.   And remember, your value add is in managing the asset- not managing your investors. If you spend all your time focusing on a problem investor- it takes your eyes off the property.

You want to attract the type of people with whom you want to work.

Once you have 10 or 15 ideal investors, the type of people with whom they hang out are probably the types of investors you want. Encourage them to bring in their friends now that they've made money with you. When I did this, before I knew it, I had six different doctors investing with me. Then I had another group of business owners and another group of accountants. It's a very organic way of growing.

This is not mass marketing. It's not accepting anybody who has money. You can be very discerning about the types of investors you allow in. When investors feel they must work to get into your deals, you know you're in that sweet spot of being a desirable person to invest with.

I should point out- once I have an investor in my deals, I treat them like gold. I want them to know if they have questions or concerns, I'm always available to discuss.

Here are a few characteristics of what I consider to be an ideal investor: they could be a business owner who nets $1 million or more a year or a professional who earns $300,000 or more per year. They should be looking for cash flowing commercial real estate and returns of 6% to 12% a year (realistic returns for real estate). They like the idea of owning commercial real estate, but they are too busy to find, negotiate, finance and execute on quality properties. They're looking for trustworthy partners to oversee their investments.

Step Four: Where Do You Find Ideal Investors?

Step four of The Five-Part Capital-Raising Framework is finding these ideal investors for your projects.

I start by building my investors' funnel, and I always start by raising money in 'concentric circles'. Who are the people closest to me with whom I have the closest relationships? Who knows, likes, and trusts me. Start there, with friends, family, and high-net-worth individuals who are in your professional groups.

Then I expand out a bit to the second group, which includes people who understand commercial real estate, as well as investing. They are looking for opportunities and have access to high-net-worth individuals. Those could be wealth-management firms, family offices, financial planners, or people dealing in private banking. They also have clients who are looking for investment opportunities.

The category 'business owners' is pretty broad. To find them in the past, I joined EO (Entrepreneurs' Organization). To be a member, your company needs to be doing a minimum of $1 million per year. That means the business owners involved are investing in themselves and are typically open to looking at new opportunities. I don't necessarily approach them directly, but it's easy to let them know what I do in natural conversation. Most people with money want to do two things: keep it and grow it. Investing in commercial real estate is generally in that plan somewhere.

Beyond EO is YPO (higher level of CEO's) and local charities. Most people who give money to a charity likely have the capacity to invest with you.

Professionals could include doctors, dentists, lawyers, accountants, and engineers; people who earn a minimum of $300,000 a year.

Next, there are individuals who influence decision-makers of high net worth individuals-mainly accountants, lawyers and bankers.

Finding connectors within a market is important. Those connectors are plugged in to their markets and network with business owners and others in the community. Just remember, your goal is to build long term relationships- not just pump people for their contacts. Play the long game.

One last area to find investors, which is something I feel is under-utilized- is commercial real estate owners. It takes some time, but you can build a database of owners in your local area. When you find opportunities close to an individual or a group of professionals that are buying, and you know this group owns other properties in the local market, it's quite possible you could do a joint venture with them. If you're savvy enough and you're able to negotiate, you can wedge yourself into the deal. It takes a little bit of legwork and some research, but it's very doable, and it's an untapped area. This is a strategy for getting yourself into much larger deals. You'll want to be sure that you have good paperwork protecting you- and make sure to deal with owners that have a solid reputation in the industry.

Chet Holmes, a master salesman I followed and who has since passed away, created a system he called **Your Dream 50 or Your Dream 100**. Simply, it is a well-defined list of investors you seek out to be your dream 50 or 100. My own personal goal, as of this writing is to create a list of 100 investors who come into my opportunities each year. The list is always changing, so I can't sit back and hope that everyone on the list today will be there in 6 months.

So, I continue to work and network to get in front of more people and let them know what I'm doing (this book is one way I will get in front of investors who might one day work with me). My goal is to add value to people I meet. Be a person people like to be around, then over time, you'll attract the ideal prospective investors.

Business owners and Professionals are so busy actively making money- they don't have a lot of time to figure out commercial real estate investing.

I know they're not investing all their money with me. Which means, they're looking at other real estate investment opportunities. So, I tell them, *"If you'd like, I can give you an unbiased perspective on how I would look at this deal, and some questions I would ask."* My goal for my investors is not to lose money- with me or with others. While I can't control other deal opportunities they come across, I can give my investors principles and rules I use that guide me in investing. I have a list of those principles at my website **www.ShaneMelanson.com** if you'd like to see them.

Summary: establish yourself as the trusted expert, the authority who's there to help those who want to invest with you in real estate. You want to be their advocate and protect them from making avoidable investment mistakes.

Step Five:
Your Deliverables

Step five is your investment deliverables.

How do you get the money?

I think this is where most new investors start, but, it's really the natural conclusion only after you've found the right property, understand the market and have relationships with ideal investors.

You will need sales collateral to start conversations with investors. I like to start with a tear sheet – which is just a **one or two pager** that summarizes the investment. It is a high-level overview, that forces you to summarize the opportunity and generates interest. Doing this upfront, will help you in presenting the deal, because often, with busy people, you only have a few minutes to get their attention. If you ramble on about how you found the property and the submarket and the brokers, etc.- you'll lose people.

It's good to have a picture or diagram of three to seven steps showing the opportunity and how you go from point A to point Z and the value you bring to the table.

I always want to have a reason to be in the deal. If I find a Class A property, in a great area – I better be prepared to explain to my investors why I'm accepting a low initial return. Investors want to know why they are giving you, the GP money. They want to see their returns before you make money. And, they generally don't get excited about 5% returns for 5 years. They can get that in liquid markets (bonds, stocks).

There should be a valid reason for you to exist in the deal, and that reason, generally is to solve a problem. And, there are many different problems but some of the obvious problems include; under market rents, higher vacancy and an opportunity to bring in a new tenant or repurpose the building to fill a gap in the market. I always have a story to tell my investors because that's how I engage them.

After the 1-2-page tear sheet comes your **pitch deck** or deck. The deck is what you show prospective investors when you are confident the property is a go. My decks are between 15 and 25 pages, but no more than 30. Your title page will have a nice picture to get their attention and a clear headline for the project.

You'll have a legal disclaimer and then a page with high level financial analysis. The 4th page is usually a compelling description of the Big Idea (Oren Klaff) – that describes the opportunity in 100 to 200 words. Then you'll discuss the problem/challenges and how you have the solution.

Next I will have detailed financial analysis with sensitivity analysis. I show what the financials are today, and then include a pro forma, which is forward looking. There should be a timeline for the property on how you plan to execute. You will have a summary of the deal structure and how investors put money into the deal (they are not cutting you cheques- they will go to your lawyer's trust account). I always end with a summary of the team, their credibility and track record

If the deal is big enough, I will set up a simple, **one-page website** investors can visit. It's not necessary, but some investors like it and it's another way they can share it with their friends. Investors love to talk about where they are putting their money- so make it easy for them to share with friends.

The website is <u>not</u> meant to market to everybody, so you should password protect it. It's a specific website your investors can visit for updates. I like to have Frequently Asked Questions and Should Ask Questions sections.

Ongoing communication is important when you're raising money. It seems many new investors trying to raise money think it's an event. It's not- it's really a process.

You're not likely to get a check during your first meeting. You're introducing the opportunity and gauging their level of interest. If they have genuine interest, you say, *"I'm not asking you for anything today other than to introduce the idea, and we can follow up once you've had an opportunity to read through the presentation."*

When I meet with an investor, I don't slap the pitch deck down first because that would be overwhelming. They would start looking at that and lose interest in me. I start with a conversation instead, and at the very end, I pass them the presentation and say, *"Here's what it looks like. You can take this away, and we can follow up in a few days to discuss if this makes sense."*

Once you've achieved a level of comfort and confidence and a track record, the conversations are natural and easy.

The investors I work with, usually ask me, *"How much are you looking for? How much do you want from me?"* Those are the questions I get now, but when you're starting, they won't be the first questions you hear. Investors will test you – to make sure you know your stuff. So be prepared for it and you must know your numbers inside and out, off the top of your head. If you need to refer to the presentation for information- you'll look unprepared and like you don't know what you're doing. Therefore I always do my underwriting- so I know the numbers inside and out.

Other documents you should prepare: The **Offering Memorandum** (OM), possibly a **Prospectus**, the **accredited investor** documentation, an **LP/GP agreement**, a **USA** (unanimous shareholders' agreement) if you have multiple general partners, or potentially a joint venture agreement. Depending on where you are investing, there could be other documents needed- these are the main ones I use to raise money. I know I've said it in the past- but it bears repeating: Hire a good lawyer who understands securities and raising money. This is not something you can skip or cheap out on. It's not cheap to have these documents prepared, but, the cost of not doing it- is being sued or jail time.

Some *nice-to-haves* collateral would include a logo and nice images to make your presentation look good.

I create my presentations in PowerPoint. They look good and professional, but I don't overdo it. HNW and ultra-wealthy are skeptical of presentations that are too fancy. If you spent 3 months and 10k building your pitch deck- what are you hiding? The deal should stand on its own. Investors look at those beautiful decks and ask (to themselves or aloud), "*Why did you spend all this time and money making this brochure so pretty? I think you're focused on the wrong thing-graphics and images, and not on the deal.*"

I made this mistake on one of the first presentations I built. I thought I had to make this professional-looking marketing piece. No one's going to tell you to your face that it's too pretty, but they'll be more skeptical if you go out of your way to make something too fancy-looking versus just going to Staples and getting a folder with aplastic, see-through cover. Slide the presentation deck in there, so it doesn't get wet or fall apart. It looks good, but it doesn't look like you are trying to over-impress them with marketing.

It's the substance of the deal you want to focus on. Spend extra time on understanding the financials and numbers of the deal.

One last observation and piece of advice I have when raising money. When it comes to the financials, many investors don't understand what they're talking about because they hire someone else to do the underwriting. When they sit down over coffee with a business owner, who reads through it, and asks about the assumptions and the numbers- the GP raising the money, can't answer the question. He (or she) is fumbling around. You look stupid and you won't raise money this way.

If the business owner is savvy at all, they will understand cash flow analysis, cash and cash returns, and return on equity. They will start to dig deep if you can't answer the basic financial questions.

Focus on the deal and financial metrics, don't worry about how pretty your presentation looks.

Experience Counts (How You can Raise Money and Invest in Commercial Real Estate Like the Wealthy)

I get there is a lot of information in this book. The goal was not to give you an A-Z detail on exactly how to raise money and invest in commercial real estate. There are entire books and courses on each of these topics alone.

It took me 10 years, full time investing in commercial real estate and raising money and being mentored by some of the best investors in Canada and the US to learn what I know today.

If you are interested in going deeper into raising money and/or investing in commercial real estate, I'd be happy to discuss your goals with you.

First, I'll help you get clear on what you are trying to achieve. I know this sounds simple and most investors start by saying- I want more money or I want to retire. Fine, but let's go deep and figure out how much you need. What resources you have now and what experience you have.

With clarity, you can start to find the right properties you want to invest in. If it makes sense, we can discuss how I can help you work through The Five Steps to raising capital and investing in commercial real estate. How I put together investment presentations. Help you with the scripts and talking points investors want to hear. We dig into the nuances of how these conversations go.

My last investment, I raised $2.7 million in a week. I'm currently working on two more opportunities, one that will require $1.9M and another larger opportunity requiring $5.7-$6.0M. I tell you this, so you know I'm actively doing this now. My business is investing in commercial real estate. But, with so many people asking me to help them- it seemed to make sense to build something that could help more investors do what I do.

When I talk to new real estate investors looking to raise money, I find many are uncomfortable asking for money. They feel like they're begging for money and have a negative emotion around asking for money.

This mindset issue is relatively easy to overcome. When I'm presenting a deal, I view it as helping my investors make money, so I'm excited. I don't see myself as a salesperson; I'm offering a valuable and in demand service. It's all mindset. It can take some time (it did for me), but once you understand what you're doing and get the reps of presenting and showing opportunities, you'll be addicted to it. It's an incredible high after a meeting with an investor who gives you a cheque for $300,000.

Once you have the mindset, you'll need to master the skills of investing and finding properties. Without the skillset of knowing how to find a property, talk to brokers, package a deal and show it to people properly- you can have the right mindset and still fall flat.

With skills and mindset in place- the last piece is execution. Finding properties and talking to investors are great- but the money is made in execution of the property. Role playing the important conversations you'll have with investors, brokers and sellers is key.

Right now, there is an opportunity for the right person, to work with me, if you want to own commercial real estate. I'm able to help people who want to raise money.

I help make sure you have the right deal.

If you can't explain to me in the first two minutes why this opportunity is a valuable one to bring to investors, then you need to stop and address things immediately. Investing in the wrong opportunity and raising money for the wrong opportunity, which I've done, is a long, slow grind.

I can help you avoid the investing pitfalls that come from years of experience. I have too many to list, but here are a few mistakes I've made: investing too far away from home, investing with the wrong partners, having the wrong general partner, buying at the wrong time, having too much leverage, including personal guarantees, etc. There are so many that this book could be as thick as a Bible, but I tried here to identify the main areas. Some people will need more help in certain areas. That's where I can guide you.

If you have questions or want more information visit me at
www.ClubSyndication.com.

Here's to your journey to true financial freedom.

Made in the USA
Middletown, DE
26 July 2019